JUST A
FRENCH MAJOR
FROM
THE BRONX

Selected cartoons from
STILL A FEW BUGS IN THE SYSTEM

JUST A FRENCH MAJOR FROM THE BRONX

a Doonesbury book

by G. B. Trudeau

POPULAR LIBRARY • NEW YORK

The cartoons in this book have appeared in newspapers in the United States and abroad under the auspices of Universal Press Syndicate.

IT'S ANOTHER DAY AT THE COLLEGE ADMISSIONS OFFICE AS ALAN, THE AMAZING ADMISSIONS OFFICER CONTINUES WITH THE TOUGH SCREENING INTERVIEWS...

AH, MRS. WASSERMAN.... COULD YOU PLEASE SEND IN THE NEXT CANDIDATE...

WOW, MARK! WHAT AN AMAZING ARTICLE! I HAD NO IDEA THE VIETNAM WAR WAS SO TERRIBLE!

WELL, DOONES, I'M GLAD THE SCALES HAVE FINALLY FALLEN FROM YOUR EYES... BUT SINCE **WHEN** HAVE YOU STARTED READING NEWSPAPERS?..

ISN'T THAT A GREAT STATUE, MIKE?.. OL' ABE LINCOLN, HE WAS REALLY SOMETHING!

OH, CALVIN!

I JUST WANT YOU TO KNOW THAT EVEN THOUGH PANTHERS ARE OUT OF VOGUE, I'M NOT SWITCHING ETHNIC GROUPS!

HAROLD
STASSEN.

ALRIGHT, WHAT'D YOU PUT IN THE CIGARETTE?..

TOUCHÉ,
YOU LITTLE
MONSTER.

...EH?

AH, GRADUATION!
THAT STIRRING CEREMONY
DURING WHICH THE
PRESIDENT LAYS OUR
DIPLOMAS ON US..

THAT'S THE NICE THING
ABOUT A SMALL COLLEGE—
IT'S SO PERSONAL.. HE'LL
PROBABLY SAY TO ME,
"GOOD WORK, LARRY, YOU'RE
A CREDIT TO THE COLLEGE!"